PLYMOUTH WARSHIPS 1900-1950

PLYMOUTH WARSHIPS

1900-1950

Syd Goodman and Iain Ballantyne

Illustrated with photographs from
The Goodman Collection

HALSGROVE

First published in Great Britain by Halsgrove, 1998

Copyright © 1998 text Syd Goodman and Iain Ballantyne

Copyright © 1998 photographs The Goodman Collection

ISBN 1 874448 82 5

Cataloguing in Publication Data
A CIP record for this title is available from the British Library

HALSGROVE
PUBLISHING, MEDIA AND DISTRIBUTION

Halsgrove House
Lower Moor Way
Tiverton, Devon, EX16 6SS
United Kingdom

Tel: 01884 243242
Fax: 01884 243325
www.halsgrove.com

Printed in Great Britain by Bookcraft (Bath) Ltd, Midsomer Norton

CONTENTS

ACKNOWLEDGEMENTS

Tha authors would like to acknowledge the assistance of the Naval History Library, the Public Relations Offices, Devonport Naval Base, and Devonport Dockyard Museum.

HMS *Snipe* arriving home at Devonport in January 1951 from the America, West Indies Station to be paid off for a refit.

Return to Devonport: HMS *Veryan Bay* coming alongside the Keyham Yard in February 1954 after service on the America, West Indies Station.

INTRODUCTION

The history of the Royal Navy and therefore the ebb and flow of Britain's fortunes as a major sea-power are inextricably linked with the Devon maritime city of Plymouth.

But, even before there was a proper British fleet, the warships of Plymouth sailed out to conquer a New World empire of riches during the Elizabethan era and defended England from the onslaught of the Spanish Armada.

The vast and glorious expanse that is Plymouth Hoe, where Sir Francis Drake played his legendary game of bowls before sallying forth to destroy the Armada in 1588, has seen so many of the great battlewagons process past either to triumph or tragedy on the seven seas.

The Royal Navy's – and therefore the British Empire's – power reached its height in the immediate aftermath of the Battle of Trafalgar in 1805.

For all but the last few years of the nineteenth century no other fleet challenged the Royal Navy's supremacy. The creation of Germany, with ambitions to dominate the seas and create and overseas empire, as the century drew to a close led to a battleship-building race that helped create the conditions for global conflict.

A whole generation of Europeans were lost in the mud and slaughter of the First World War's land combat stalemate while the dreadnoughts of Britain and Germany clashed inconclusively at Jutland in May 1916.

Some of the Plymouth-built battleships of the First World War were to live on to serve in the Second World War, by which time the contenders for the Royal Navy's crown were multiplying alarmingly.

The Japanese and Americans, as well as a remilitarized Germany and resurgent Italy, showed the world that Britannia could not always be certain of ruling the waves.

But still the British fleet was a powerful force, not conceding its time of supremacy had passed until the 1950s.

Throughout that most glorious era of British sea-power, stretching from Trafalgar to the Second World War, the people of Plymouth suffered the naval calamities and took joy in the triumphs as no other city in the British Isles could, not even hallowed Portsmouth.

Devonport Dockyard, which to this day is the engineering powerhouse of the South West economy and the modern Royal Navy, built the ships while the city provided many of the sailors. Their families waved them away from the Hoe and Devil's Point to imperial patrols on the other side of the globe and waited patiently, for months if not years, for them to return from the great battles.

A heavy price was paid in Plymothian blood at Jutland, despite its inconclusiveness, and in the early naval disasters of the Second World War. The city itself was devastated by Luftwaffe bombers attempting to destroy the Royal Navy's most important base.

This book chronicles the history of the British fleet during its golden era through photographs – many of them never before published – of Plymouth warships and in that way pays tribute to one of the world's most famous maritime communities.

We see sail give way to steam, which moves aside for diesel engines, which in turn makes way for gas turbines and petrol engines.

The shape and grace of the warships was dictated mercilessly by the gigantic strides in propulsion. Advances in weapons – from cannons to massive, rifled, breech-loading guns and torpedoes plus the warplanes which carried them – also took place, again shaping the lines of the fleet's warships and creating radically new types of vessels.

Men o' war gave way to ironclads, battleships found they were challenged by tiny, impudent submarines, by destroyers and aircraft carriers. Cruisers and battle cruisers played supporting roles to the glamour stars of the fleet and often suffered the worst casualties.

We chart the careers of them all – the big, the beautiful, the ugly and the small.

In this book we have tried to show that the variety of warship design was the spice of a vibrant seafaring life.

For those who survive as witnesses to the history in these pages, or their families and friends, many of the photographs will bring memories flooding back. For ships were not just dead metal and rivets, they were floating towns, each with enough stories to keep a soap opera going for centuries. When an old sailor looks at the ship which he lived in for years, he sees all his mates, all the scrapes and the lucky escapes they were involved in, all the terrors of naval warfare they had to face.

Many Plymouth sailors are not here to reflect on what the warships meant, because they made the ultimate sacrifice. In those cases the photograph of a warship, passing out to sea with her crew parading on deck, is a fitting memorial.

It is horrifying, yet fascinating, to discover how many of the sturdy, tough vessels in this book met a cruel fate; it reminds us that the Royal Navy was twice in the first half of this century involved in waging a sustained, and bitter, battle to save this island nation from aggressors.

Of course, the story of Plymouth and her warships didn't stop where this book ends – in the early 1950s – for the Royal Navy has fought two more naval wars since, in the South Atlantic in 1982 and the Persian Gulf in 1991, and also played a crucial role in UN operations off the former Yugoslavia during the savage civil wars in the Balkans (between 1992 and 1996).

The comrades who have survived the two world wars, and all the other conflicts of the twentieth century, still get together all over the UK, and in all four corners of the world, to toast their old ships and those that didn't return.

While it is by no means a comprehensive chronicle of every single event that happened in the life of every single ship, this book is, we hope, a fitting salute to a Royal Navy which has protected Britain well for more than 300 years.

Syd Goodman and Iain Ballantyne

THE WARSHIPS

HMS *St Vincent*

Laid down at Devonport Dockyard in May 1810, she was launched on 11 March 1815, the largest 'wooden wall' (man o' war) to be built at Devonport. Her displacement was 4672 tons. For many years she lay in reserve until, in 1831, she commissioned for service with the Mediterranean Fleet. In 1862 HMS *St Vincent* became a boy sailors' training ship, moored off Haslar Creek, Portsmouth. She was paid off for disposal on 12 January 1906. On 15 May 1906 she was auctioned at No. 3 Store at Devonport Dockyard and sold to M/S (Marine Stores) Castles of London for £5,350. She was towed from Portsmouth to Falmouth, where she arrived on 23 June 1906. During that weekend she was open to the public (price of admission 3d. per head); the monies received went to naval charities. With the open weekend over, the job of breaking her up began.

HMS *Defiance*

HMS *Defiance* has long been a naval title associated with Plymouth, her name being used for shore-based engineering establishments. Pictured here (right) moored off Saltash, *Defiance* was built in 1861. Also in the photograph are HMS *Cleopatra* (centre foreground), built in 1878, and HMS *Spartan* (left), built in 1891. HMS *Defiance* was notable for being the first naval establishment to receive a Morse code transmission in the late 1890s, when *Defiance* was being used as home for a torpedo school.

HMS *Rattlesnake*

Built by Chatham Dockyard and completed in 1862, *Rattlesnake* was a wooden sail and steam corvette. From 1868 to 1869 she was flagship of the West Africa Squadron. She was broken up at Devonport Dockyard in 1882.

HMS *Condor*

A 'composite gun vessel' launched at Devonport Dockyard in December 1877, her first commission took her to the Mediterranean, where she spent the next ten years. In 1882, under the command of Lord Charles Beresford, she took part in the bombardment of Alexandria, which was in response to the massacre of Europeans in Egypt during a revolt against British and French interference in the country's affairs. HMS *Condor* returned to Devonport in 1877, was paid off and sold in 1889 to G. Cohen & Son, London, to be broken up.

HMS *Racoon*

Completed at Devonport in 1888, she was to serve on the Cape of Good Hope and West Coast of Africa stations until 1897, when she returned home to be paid off into the reserve. In 1896 she had taken part in the bombardment of the Royal Palace at Zanzibar to subdue an anti-British, and possibly pro-German, sultan. Placed on the sales list in 1904, she was sold for £4,150 to G. Cohen & Son, London, in 1905 and broken up.

HMS *Leander*

Completed in 1885, she served on the China and Pacific stations, then was converted to a destroyer depot ship, serving on the Atlantic, Mediterranean and Nore Stations. She was sold in 1920 to Castles of Plymouth and broken up.

HMS *Edgar*

A First Class cruiser built by Devonport Dockyard and, on completion in the early 1890s, the largest warship ever built there at the time, she supported the army landings at Gallipoli in the Dardanelles during the First World War. She was later used as a training and harbour duties guardship. Placed on the disposal list, she was sold to T.W. Ward and broken up at Morecambe in 1923.

HMS *Speedwell*

A torpedo gunboat built at Devonport in 1889, during the First World War she served as a minesweeper. After the war she was paid off, then sold to the Cornish Salvage Company and broken up at Ilfracombe, arriving there in March 1920.

HMS *Philomel*

Launched in 1890 at Devonport, she was to serve the Royal Navy and the Royal New Zealand Navy for over half a century. Another participant in the 1896 bombardment of Zanzibar, during the First World War she took part in the hunt for the German raider *Emden* in the Far East before being paid off in 1917 and becoming a training ship at Devonport Naval Base, New Zealand (until 1946). In 1947 she went to Coromandel to be stripped, with her hulk scuttled off there in 1949.

HMS *Sirius*

Completed in 1891, she served on a variety of stations until 1918, when she was prepared at Chatham Dockyard as a blockship and 'expended' at Ostende in April 1918: she was scuttled in the mouth of the harbour to prevent it being used as a base for German naval operations.

HMS *Pique*

Built by Palmers, Jarrow, on completion in 1892 she arrived at Devonport and was held in reserve until 1895. She then went to China, returning home in 1898. She sailed for China once more shortly afterwards, serving there until 1903. On returning home again she was placed in reserve and laid up until 1911, when she was sold to F.E. Rudge and broken up.

HMS *Retribution*

An Apollo Class cruiser, of which 20 were built, she was one of eight members of the class disposed of between 1910 and 1914. This photograph has particular interest as the buildings in the background at South Yard were to be destroyed by enemy bombing during the Second World War.

HMS *Sybille*

Completed by Stephenson, Newcastle, in 1892, from completion until 1900 she served at Devonport, Portsmouth and in the Mediterranean. In 1900 she sailed for the Cape, where, on 16 January 1901, she was wrecked in Lambert's Bay.

HMS *Resolution*

A Royal Sovereign Class battleship, built by Palmers and launched in May 1892, she is seen here at anchor off Torpoint. The seven ships of her class initially suffered from excessive rolling in heavy seas. HMS *Resolution* was to experience such savage rolling in the Bay of Biscay during one voyage early in her life that her captain ordered her turned around and back to port. He demanded action to cure the rolling and got it: all the Royal Sovereign Class battleships were given bilge keels to make them more stable. The *Resolution* served with the Mediterranean and Channel Fleets until 1914, when she was paid off to be broken up in Holland.

HMS *St George*

Completed in 1894, she had a long and active life as a cruiser, boys' training ship, destroyer depot ship and submarine depot ship until she was sold in 1920 to Castles of Plymouth and broken up.

HMS *Bonaventure*

Early service took her to the China Station and the Pacific. On returning home she was fitted out as a sea-going base ship for submarines. The First World War saw her used as a depot ship in home and Mediterranean waters. Paid off after the war, she was sold in 1920 and broken up at Bo'ness.

HMS *Theseus*

A sister ship to the *St George*, HMS *Theseus* was completed in 1896. Her service life took her to the Mediterranean, the North Sea, the Dardanelles and the Black Sea until she became a depot ship for trawlers pressed into Admiralty service. Sold in 1921 to the Slough Trading Company, she was broken up in Germany.

HMS *Fox*

A cruiser launched in 1893, she was to spend many years in Middle Eastern waters. In the First World War she took part in the bombardment of Somaliland and other operations off the east coast of Africa, including the bombardment of Illij and Dar-es-Salaam in 1917. She was sold in 1920 to Cardiff Marine Stores and broken up. It was a photograph of HMS *Fox* that started the Goodman Collection, as Syd Goodman's grandfather served on this ship.

HMS *Hermione*

Laid down at Devonport Dockyard in 1891 and commissioned in 1895, this cruiser saw service in home and foreign waters, during which time she took part in early trials to assess the viability of operating aircraft from ships. Sold to the shipbreakers in 1921, she was purchased and converted to a boys' training ship, her new lease of life lasting until 1940, when she was sold to T.W. Ward and broken up at Gravesend.

HMS *Talbot*

A cruiser launched at Devonport in April 1895, her first commission was to the North America, West Indies Station and she came under fire from the Americans during the Spanish-American war of 1898. In 1914, as a member of the 12th Cruiser Squadron, she escorted Canadian troops carried in 32 liners to Plymouth. They had been diverted from Southampton because of U-boat activity in the Channel. She was sold in 1921 to the Multilocular Shipbreaking Company and broken up.

HMS *Andromeda*

Built at Pembroke Dockyard, she was a Diadem Class cruiser with an 11,000-ton displacement and was completed in September 1899. Her first commission took her to the Mediterranean until 1902, when she returned home and spent two years in refit. On completion of this she went to the China Station. HMS *Andromeda* returned home after two years and then spent many years with a nucleus crew at Chatham and Devonport. During 1913 she became a boys' training ship at Devonport. In 1919 she was renamed *Impregnable* and became part of the HMS *Defiance* torpedo training school. She remained part of *Defiance* until August 1956, when she left Devonport under tow, bound for Belgium and the breakers.

HMS *Highflyer*

Completed in 1900, her claim to fame in the First World War was that she disabled the German armed merchant cruiser *Kaiser Wilhelm der Grosse* in 1914. The *Kaiser Wilhelm* scuttled herself. As a liner the German vessel had been a frequent caller at Plymouth before the war. HMS *Highflyer* was paid off in 1919 and sold at Bombay in 1921 for breaking up.

HMS Good Hope

A Drake Class cruiser completed in 1902, she served with the Channel, Atlantic, Mediterranean and Grand fleets. She went to the South Atlantic as flagship of Rear Admiral Sir Christopher Cradock. During the Battle of Coronel in late 1914 she blew up with the loss of all hands.

HMS Bedford

A Monmouth Class cruiser built in 1901 for duties on the empire's trade routes. While on deployment to the China Station in August 1910 she was wrecked in the Korean Sea.

HMS *Forth*

Built as a Second Class cruiser in 1904, she became a depot ship for submarines during the First World War. She served as such until 1920, when she was paid off and sold in 1921 to be broken up in Germany.

HMS *Hogue*

Completed in 1902, HMS *Hogue* was a Bacchante Class cruiser. Early on 22 September 1914, while she was on patrol in the North Sea with sister ships HMS *Aboukir* and *Cressy*, an explosion rent the *Aboukir*, which then began to sink. *Hogue* and *Cressy* went to her aid, only to be torpedoed by U9, which had been patiently stalking all three obsolete warships. It was one of the worst disasters to befall the Royal Navy in the First World War, with 1459 British sailors losing their lives. Only days before, the order to withdraw the aged trio from service had been issued, but it had yet to be enforced at the time of their voyage to disaster.

HMS *King Edward VII*

Name ship of a class of battleships, she was launched at Devonport Dockyard in July 1903. On launching her, King Edward VII decreed that she should always be a flagship. She was the first battleship to use the new docks at Gibraltar. In 1916, while en route from Scapa Flow to Belfast to undergo a refit, she struck a mine off Cape Wrath. Heavy weather meant it was not possible to establish an effective tow. Her crew was taken off by the four destroyers escorting her and a few hours later she turned turtle and sank.

HMS *Cornwallis*

A cruiser built by Thames Iron Works and launched in July 1901, she was to be sunk in the First World War. In January 1917 she was steaming off Malta when she was struck by torpedoes from U*32*.

HMS *Temeraire*

A Bellerophon Class battleship built at Devonport Dockyard and launched in August 1907, her completion was delayed due to an engineering strike. She served at the Battle of Jutland in 1916, survived undamaged and was paid off into the reserve fleet in 1919. She then became a sea-going training ship. In 1921 she was paid off and sold to the Stanlee Shipbreaking Company, Dover, arriving there in 1922 to be broken up.

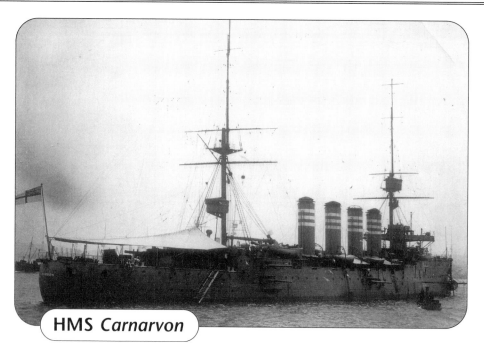

HMS *Carnarvon*

Completed in May 1905, this cruiser was to serve on the South Atlantic, Atlantic and North America, West Indies stations. During December 1914 she took part in the Battle of the Falklands. From 1919 to 1921 she served as a cadets' training ship, then was sold to the Slough Trading Company and broken up in Germany.

HMS *Minotaur*

Name ship of a class of cruisers, she was launched at Devonport in 1906. While under trials in Plymouth Sound and at anchor, there was an explosion in which five of her crew were injured. In August 1914 she sank the German vessel SS *Elsbeth*. She later saw action in the North Sea and took part in the Battle of Jutland. Paid off for disposal in 1919, she was sold to T.W. Ward and broken up at Milford Haven.

HMS *Vanguard*

A St Vincent Class battleship launched in 1909 and completed in less than two years, she was the most cheaply built battleship of her era. While at anchor in Scapa Flow on 9 July 1917 she blew up, with the loss of 804 crew members. Only two sailors aboard her at the time of the explosion survived, and the only other living members of her crew were several officers who had been visiting a neighbouring ship. The explosion which destroyed her was so powerful it hurled one of her lifeboats a distance of seven miles. The cause of this catastrophe was deemed to be faulty ammunition. The wreck was raised in 1927 and towed to the Tyne for breaking up.

HMS *Argyll*

Launched in 1904, she served with the 1st Cruiser Squadron and also acted as guardship to the Royal Yacht while the king was being conveyed to India in 1911/12. On 28 October 1915 she was stranded on the Bell Rock off the East Coast of Scotland and was lost.

HMS *Liverpool*

Completed in 1910, she served with the Grand Fleet and in the Mediterranean. Placed in reserve at Devonport in 1919, she was then sold to the Slough Trading Company and broken up in Germany.

HMS *Centurion*

Built at Devonport, she was to serve in both world wars. Between the wars she was fitted out as a radio-controlled target ship. In 1941 she was disguised as HMS *Anson*, a modern King George V Class battle-ship, to mislead enemy intelligence over the movements of the real thing. After this she served as an anti-aircraft escort ship on convoys in the Mediterranean, suffering some damage during air attacks. By 1944 she was back at Devonport being fitted out for her last duty: she was to be sunk off Omaha Beach, Normandy, to form part of a harbour for landing supplies across the beachhead after the 6 June D-Day landings.

HMS *Thunderer*

An Orion Class super dreadnought, completed in 1912 and the last large warship to be built by the Thames Iron Works (Blackwall). Like other ships of the class, HMS *Thunderer* saw action at Jutland, as part of the Second Battle Squadron, and came through unharmed. By 1920 she was a cadets' training ship. She was paid off and sold for breaking up in 1926. The name HMS *Thunderer* lived on as the title of the Royal Naval Engineering College at Manadon in Plymouth until the mid-1990s, when it was shut as part of post-Cold War defence cuts.

HMS *Lion*

Built at Devonport, the battle cruiser *Lion* was to become famous as Admiral David Beatty's flagship during the First World War. She saw action at the battles of Heligoland Bight, Dogger Bank and Jutland. She was damaged at both Jutland and Dogger Bank. In 1920 she was paid off into the reserve and sold for breaking up at Hebburn, Co. Durham. She was cut in two and the stern section, while under tow to Blyth, broke free from its tugs as if seeking a more dignified death at sea. But it was reconnected and joined the rest of the warship in the breaker's yard.

HMS *New Zealand*

The construction of the battle cruiser HMS *New Zealand* was funded by the New Zealand Government as its contribution to building up the Royal Navy in the face of the German threat. She commissioned for service on 12 November 1912 under Captain Lionel Halsey, RN. In January 1915 she took part in the Battle of Dogger Bank. Involved in a collision at sea with HMS *Australia* in April 1916, she was, however, sufficiently repaired by May to take part in the Battle of Jutland, where she sustained slight damage. The Maori people presented HMS *New Zealand* with a cloak and a talisman called a 'tiki' which the captain wore each time she went into battle. She came through each time unscathed. During the war years she steamed 84,458 miles and burned 97,034 tons of coal. She was retired from service in 1922 as part of the Royal Navy's compliance with the Washington Treaty of that year which sought to restrict the size of the world's fleets.

HMS *Warspite*

Possibly Plymouth's most famous battleship, HMS *Warspite* was launched in 1913 and was to fight in both world wars. *Warspite* was badly damaged at Jutland, being hit by more than a dozen large-calibre German shells. At one point during the clash her engine room was flooded and her steering jammed. For some time she could do nothing but circle, making a easy target for German battleships. Peacetime was no better for her: in 1928 she struck a reef in the Aegean; in 1933 she collided with a steamer off the mouth of the River Tagus. After reconstruction, between 1933 and 1936, she was to find her finest hours during the Second World War. Seeing action at the battles of Narvik, Matapan and supporting the Normandy and Walcheren landings in North West Europe, she acquired an enduring reputation as a lucky survivor. She took it and gave it, winning more battle honours than any other British warship in the Second World War.

During the evacuation of Crete in May 1941 she was badly damaged by bombs from Luftwaffe Stuka dive-bombers. Following extensive repairs in an American shipyards she returned to the fray in 1943 and, while supporting Allied troops landing at Salerno, Italy, was hit by a radio-controlled bomb. Interim repairs were carried out, enabling her to give gunfire support to the Normandy landings in June 1944. However, she sustained further damage during this operation from a magnetic mine. After repairs she used her guns to back up the invasion of the Dutch island of Walcheren in November 1944, the last major amphibious operation by Allied troops in North West Europe. She was retired from active service in early 1945. Reduced to the Reserve Fleet in 1945, she was sold off for scrap in 1946.

In April 1947, while en route to the breaker's yard, she parted her tow off the Cornish Coast and ran aground at Prussia Cove, where she was partially broken up. Her hull was then beached near St Michael's Mount and she was finally demolished in 1956.

HMS *Dublin*

Completed in March 1913, on the outbreak of war she was serving in the Mediterranean. She took part in the unsuccessful pursuit of the German raiders *Goeben* and *Breslau* in the Mediterranean. On her return to home waters she was present at Jutland and later in 1916 came under attack from a German submarine and sustained some serious damage. Withdrawn from service and placed on the disposal list, she was sold in 1926 to M/S King & Son, Garston, Liverpool, and broken up.

HMS *Gabriel*

A Marksman Class destroyer completed in 1916, HMS *Gabriel* was to have a short life, owing to defence cutbacks. Sold in 1921 to M/S Wards, she was broken up at Lelant.

HMS *Eagle*

Construction of the *Eagle*, laid down as a battleship for Chile, was suspended and she was purchased by the Royal Navy in 1917. She was completed as an aircraft carrier. During the Second World War, carrying Swordfish torpedo bombers, she operated in the Mediterranean. On 11 August 1942, while taking part in the Operation Pedestal convoy to Malta, she was torpedoed north of the Algerian coast by U73 and sank.

HMS *Tiger*

Completed in 1914, this battle cruiser was that time the largest and fastest ship in the fleet. She was also the last coal-burning ship built for the Royal Navy. She was present at the battles of Dogger Bank and Jutland. After the war she became a training ship at Devonport until 1931, when she was sold to M/S Wards and broken up at Inverkeithing.

HMS *Royal Oak*

Built at Devonport Dockyard and launched in November 1914, this 'R' Class battleship served in the First World War but was to be tragically lost within weeks of the beginning of the Second World War. She saw service in the Home, Atlantic and Mediterranean fleets. In 1937, while enforcing a League of Nations blockade during the Spanish Civil War, she was attacked by dive-bombers belonging to one of the warring factions. In 1938 she carried the body of Queen Maud of Norway home from Portsmouth to Oslo for burial. *Royal Oak* was sunk at anchor in Scapa Flow after a U-boat managed to penetrate defences in October 1939. Three torpedoes hit her and 833 of her crew died in a massive explosion.

HMS *Agincourt*

The battleship HMS *Agincourt* was built by Armstrong Whitworth and launched in January 1913, begin-ning life as the *Rio de Janeiro*, for the Brazilian Navy. But she was then bought, in a convoluted deal, by a Turkish sultan. However, while she was still being completed the First World War broke out, with Turkey on the enemy side. Taken over by the Royal Navy in 1914 and named HMS *Agincourt*, she mounted the largest number of big-calibre guns ever fitted to a Royal Navy warship: fourteen 12-inch guns in seven turrets. Officially her turrets were named A, B, P, Q, X, Y and Z but it was well known within the fleet that they were more commonly referred to by the names of the days of the week. HMS *Agincourt*'s war service included the Battle of Jutland, where she fired 144 shells, scoring more than a dozen hits on German warships. Paid off in 1919, she lay discarded until used for experimental work. She was sold off and broken up Rosyth Shipbreaking Company, arriving there in 1922.

HMS *Valiant*

Another battleship which served in two world wars and was present at Jutland, between the wars HMS *Valiant* was modernized. During the Second World War she was sent to the Mediterranean. She was one of the escorts that took part of the Italian fleet to Malta when it surrendered in 1943. She then went to the Eastern Fleet and while at Trincomalee, Ceylon, she was badly damaged below the waterline when the floating dock she was in collapsed. She returned to the UK via the Cape and anchored at Devonport, where she became a stokers' harbour training ship. The two photographs here show her as a ocean-going battleship and as a training ship moored in the River Tamar. In 1948 she went to Cairnryan to be cut down before moving to Troon in 1950 for final demolition.

The submarine *J.7* is pictured here about to be launched on 21 February 1917 in the historic Covered Slip at the dockyard's South Yard. The submarine was transferred to the Royal Australian Navy in 1919 and, on being retired from service a decade later, sold to Morris and Watt of Melbourne. Her hull was scuttled at Hampton, Victoria in 1930.

A light cruiser is pictured in dry dock at Devonport during the First World War for repairs to battle damage.

An early photograph of Morice Yard with a cruiser, destroyers and an auxiliary in the river. The Royal Navy van in the foreground dates this photograph as early twentieth century. The oil fuel tanks behind the three-funnelled cruiser are at Thanckes, Torpoint. It is still in use as a fuel depot today.

HMS *Menelaus*

Launched in 1915 as a monitor called M*31*, she was to be converted to a minelayer in 1919 and later renamed *Melpomene*. She subsequently became a tender to torpedo training school HMS *Defiance* at Devonport and was renamed *Menelaus* in 1940. The picture shows her with a torpedo tube fitted over her bow. In 1948 she was towed to M/S Rees of Llanelli and broken up.

HMS *Repulse*

A battle cruiser completed in 1916, she was to undergo extensive modernization between the wars. After some Atlantic convoy work during the early part of the Second World War, HMS *Repulse* was sent to the Far East in late 1941, in company with the brand new battleship HMS *Prince of Wales*. Their despatch to the Far East was an ill-judged attempt to use gunboat diplomacy to stave off Japanese aggression against British colonies – Malaysia and Singapore in particular. It was hoped that the presence of the two capital ships in the region would prevent Japanese troop landings on the Malay Peninsula. Three days after the 7 December sneak attack on Pearl Harbor Japanese carrier aircraft pounced on HMS *Repulse* and HMS *Prince of Wales* as they steamed in the Gulf of Siam. Both warships went to the bottom, *Repulse* taking more than half her crew with her.

HMS *Titania*

Purchased in 1915, she became a depot ship for submarines as seen here, with *G4* and *G10* alongside. She served until 1948, when she was sent to be broken up at Faslane.

HMS *Ramillies*

An 'R' Class battleship that served in both world wars. During the Second World War she was part of the task force which occupied the island of Madagascar and in June of the same year (1942) she was torpedoed by an enemy submarine and had to sail to Durban for repairs. In June 1944 she provided bombardment support for the Normandy landings and then covering fire for the Allied invasion of southern France. Her last days were spent as a harbour training ship, and in February 1948 she was sent to be broken up at Cairnryan.

HMS *Torrid*

A destroyer completed in 1917, she spent many years in reserve until she was handed over to shipbreakers in part payment for the ex-liner *Majestic* in 1937. The Royal Navy wanted to use the latter as an accommodation ship, but she had been sent to the breaker's yard at Inverkeithing. A deal to retrieve *Majestic* was struck which entailed giving the breakers the equivalent tonnage of warships surplus to requirements. HMS *Torrid* was one of these exchange vessels. While en route to Scotland she ran aground at Trefusis Point in Cornwall and ended up being broken up where she lay.

HMS *Hood*

When they were ordered, *Hood* and her three sister ships were to be the battle cruisers to beat all battle cruisers. But lessons learnt at the Battle of Jutland – where the Royal Navy suffered dramatic battle cruiser losses due to inadequate armour protection – saw her three sisters cancelled. *Hood* was too far advanced to cancel, but did have 5000 tons of additional armour fitted in an attempt to give her better protection against a Jutland-style calamity.

Once completed, HMS *Hood* was hailed as one of the most beautiful warships ever built and her 41,200 tons made her one of the biggest in naval history. She was extremely swift too, capable of more than 30 knots. In the 1920s she sailed the globe as an ambassador of British imperial power. During the 1930s a rebuilding programme was projected, but the Second World War arrived before it was carried out. *Hood* first fired her guns in anger at Oran, during the Royal Navy's reluctant destruction of the Vichy French fleet. She next let rip with her 15-inch guns during the fateful clash with the German battleship *Bismarck* in late May 1941.

Hood and the brand new King George V Class battleship HMS *Prince of Wales* had sailed out to search for the *Bismarck* in the Denmark Straits. Unfortunately, deadly accurate German gunnery and her thin upper armour led to a disaster exactly like the one that befell the battle cruisers at Jutland 24 years before: the *Hood* was blown apart when a shell sliced deep into her interior and ignited an ammunition magazine. Of her 1419 crew, only three survived.

HMS *Rodney*

The shocking loss of 'The Mighty *Hood*' was to be avenged by the battleship HMS *Rodney*, which played a crucial role in destroying the *Bismarck* a few days later. Built under the restrictions of the Washington Treaty of 1922, which sought to preserve peace by limiting the tonnage of the world's leading fleets, *Rodney* and her sister ship HMS *Nelson* had odd, truncated hulls to save on weight. Their three gun turrets – carrying a devastating nine 16-inch guns (the biggest-calibre guns ever carried by Royal Navy battlewagons) – were placed forward of the main superstructure. During the inter-war years HMS *Rodney* became a regular star attraction of Navy Weeks at Devonport (as pictured here) and also in Plymouth Sound.

HMS *Rodney*

This photograph shows *Rodney* with *Hood* behind about to pass Plymouth Pier.

Both robust and formidable, *Rodney* and *Nelson* gave sterling service during the Second World War. HMS *Rodney* was on convoy escort duty in late May 1941 when she was ordered to take part in the hunt for the German battleship *Bismarck*, teaming up with the KGV Class battleship HMS *King George V*. Accompanied by cruisers and aircraft carriers, they soon cornered the German battleship, with *Rodney*'s gunnery rapidly proving superior to that of the *Bismarck*. She scored a crucial hit which wiped out the *Bismarck*'s bridge and robbed her of effective gunnery control. *Rodney* also hastened *Bismarck*'s end by hitting her with a torpedo – the only time in the history of naval warfare that a battleship attacked and hit another with a torpedo.

HMS *Rodney* used her guns to give fire-power support to the Allied landings at Sicily, on mainland Italy and Normandy before being put into reserve at the end of the war. She was broken up at Inverkeithing, arriving there in 1948.

HMS *Emerald*

An 'E' Class cruiser launched in May 1920, she first arrived at Devonport for refitting in 1931. On completion she returned to the 4th Cruiser Squadron. In 1939 she was a boys' training ship at Chatham and was then recommissioned for front-line service. October 1939 saw her leave Plymouth carrying gold bullion to pay the Americans for war materiel, a job she was to perform many times, in addition to escort, bombardment and convoy duties. She was broken up at Troon in 1948.

HMS *Adventure*

Launched at Devonport Dockyard in June 1924, she was the first Royal Navy ship to use diesel engines. Officially termed a cruiser-minelayer, she was used in a variety of roles. In the early days of the Second World War, while returning to Chatham, she hit a mine in the Thames Estuary and sustained significant damage. She was damaged again by a mine during passage from Milford Haven to Liverpool. In the spring of 1943 she ran down a German merchant vessel and forced her to scuttle. In 1944 she was converted to a landing-craft repair ship and took part in the Normandy landings. She was broken up in 1947 by M/S Ward at Briton Ferry.

Fleet Auxiliary *Olna*

Launched in 1921, *Olna* was built in accordance with the Colwyn Committee's recommendations that surplus dockyard facilities should be used to construct merchant ships. She had a chequered life: in 1931, while off Canada, she collided with a merchant ship, and a few years later she ran aground off Ceylon. In May 1941 she was bombed and set on fire in Suda Bay by German aircraft and lost.

HMS *Frobisher*

Built at Devonport Dockyard and completed in 1924, HMS *Frobisher*'s pre-war service was varied. During the Second World War she served with the Home and Eastern fleets. In August 1944, while off the Normandy beachhead, she sustained serious damage after being torpedoed by a marauding German E-boat. On completion of repairs she became a cadets' training ship, then was paid off. She was broken up at Newport in 1949.

HMS *Berwick*

A Kent Class cruiser, completed in 1928, she saw a fair amount of action in the Second World War. In late November 1940 she was damaged during a sea battle off Sardinia between the Royal Navy's Gibraltar-based Force H, led by the battle cruiser HMS *Renown*, and an Italian force of seven heavy cruisers and two battleships. The following month HMS *Berwick* was again damaged when she traded shots with the German cruiser *Admiral Hipper* while protecting a convoy in the Atlantic. After repairs lasting several months she took up convoy escort duties on the north Russia run. She was used for trooping duties to the Far East in 1945/46. HMS *Berwick* arrived at Blyth in 1948 to be broken up by M/S Hughes Bolckow.

HMS *Courageous*

Built as a large light battle cruiser, she underwent conversion to an aircraft carrier at Devonport Dockyard. As naval aircraft technology was advancing at a rapid pace it was a case of trial and error until the carrier as we see her in the photograph emerged. At the outbreak of the Second World War she was serving with the Home Fleet and while on patrol off Ireland on 17 September 1939 was sunk by U29.

HMS *Curaçao*

Completed in 1918, she served with the 5th Light Cruiser Squadron, later becoming the flagship of the 1st Cruiser Squadron, Atlantic Fleet. During the Second World War, while escorting the *Queen Mary* carrying troops, she was accidentally rammed and sunk by the Cunard liner.

HMS *Erebus*

Launched in June 1916 as the monitor M*15*, she was later named *Erebus*. During the Second World War her guns were used to great effect during shore bombardment at Sicily, Calais, Dunkirk, Le Havre and Walcheren. Placed in reserve, then sold in 1946, she was broken up at Inverkeithing.

HMBDV *Nordland*

Built in 1916, one of many vessels requisitioned from the fishing fleets, she was taken under Royal Navy command in February 1940 and converted for duties as a boom defence vessel (as pictured here in Plymouth Sound). She was returned to her owners in 1946.

HMS *Colombo*

Commissioned for service in 1919, she spent her early life on the East Indies and China Stations. On the outbreak of war in 1939 she was the flagship of the 11th Cruiser Squadron, Reserve Fleet. She underwent conversion to an anti-aircraft cruiser and served with the Mediterranean Fleet. Reduced to Reserve Fleet status again in 1945, she was laid up in the River Fal until January 1948, when she was sent to Cashmores at Newport for demolition.

HMS *Delhi*

Completed in 1919, she was commissioned for service with the 1st Light Cruiser Squadron at Devonport. After service on many stations she was reduced to the Reserve at Devonport in 1938. However, she was reactivated for the Second World War. In 1942 she was badly damaged after coming under air attack in Algiers Bay. HMS *Delhi* was badly damaged again in February 1945: while anchored in Split, on the Dalmatian coast, she was targeted by German attack boats and had to be towed home to the United Kingdom. She was then placed in reserve at Dartmouth. She arrived at Cashmores in Newport to be broken up in March 1948.

HMS *Hermes*

Launched at Elswick in 1919, and the first ship purposely designed as an aircraft carrier, she was towed to Devonport for completion. She could carry a dozen aircraft in her hanger, with a further ten aboard in storage ready be swiftly brought into service. HMS *Hermes* served on training duties until 1939, when she joined the Home Fleet. She was then sent to the Far East. Joining the Eastern Fleet, she was attacked by Japanese aircraft on 9 April 1942 off Ceylon and sunk.

HMS *Diomede*

Loaned to the Royal New Zealand Navy in 1925, she was handed back to the Royal Navy in 1936. She arrived back at Devonport in 1938 under tow for service as a boy sailors' training ship. After war service she returned to training duties in 1944. In 1945 she was placed in reserve at Falmouth. She was sold in 1946 and while under tow to the breaker's yard at Dalmuir she grounded off Penzance. Refloated the next day, she continued her journey, arriving at Arnotts Young's on 13 May 1946 to be broken up.

HMS *Carlisle*

A 'C' Class cruiser completed in 1918, between the wars she served on many stations and was modernized in 1939. During the Second World War she was damaged while taking part in the 1941 evacuation of Crete. In the disastrous Aegean campaign of 1943 she was caught by Luftwaffe dive-bombers and severely damaged. She had to be towed to Alexandria, where she was used as a base ship. She was hulked until 1948, when she was broken up.

HMS *Sutton*

Launched in 1918, she was a Hunt Class minesweeper and a coal burner. In 1939 she was serving in the Mediterranean but returned to home waters in December of that year. She took part in the Dunkirk evacuation and also supported the Normandy landings. Paid off into reserve, she was sold to M/S Dohmen and Habets and arrived in Belgium in July 1947 to be broken up.

HMT *Moonrise*

One of the many trawlers requisitioned by the Royal Navy and used in a variety of roles. Taken over in 1940, she was based at Plymouth and used on minesweeping and patrol duties. She was handed back to her owners in 1946.

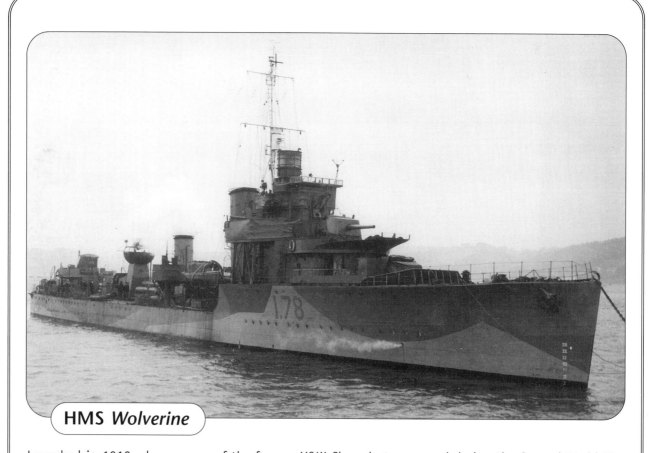

HMS *Wolverine*

Launched in 1919, she was one of the famous V&W Class destroyers and during the Second World War was converted to a short-range escort. In August 1942, while escorting HMS *Furious* in the Mediterranean, she rammed and sank the Italian submarine *Dagabur*. Placed in reserve in 1945, she was sent to Troon in January 1946 to be broken up.

HMS *Watchman*

Ordered under the 1916 emergency war programme, she was completed in 1918. Twenty years later she took part in another war. She was based at Plymouth in 1944 and during this time attacked E-boats in Lyme Bay and sank U*1195* in the Channel. Paid off in July 1945, HMS *Watchman* was broken up at Inverkeithing.

HMS *Vansittart*

Built by Beardmore and launched in April 1919, like many of her sisters she served on many stations between the wars. In 1943 she was converted at Middlesbrough to a long-range escort. She is pictured here in Plymouth Sound just after completion of that conversion. In 1946 she was taken over by the British Iron and Steel Corporation and broken up by Cashmores at Newport.

HMS *Cumberland*

A Kent Class cruiser completed in 1928, she served in many theatres of war. In 1940 she was damaged by a shell from a shore battery druing the Dakar operation which sought to neutralize Vichy French forces and capture the West African port for use as an Allied base. From 1945 to 1946 *Cumberland* was also used for trooping duties to the Far East, then reduced to the reserve and subsequently underwent conversion to a trials cruiser. She damaged her bottom in Plymouth Sound shortly after the Second World War when she tried to go to sea through the eastern side of the Plymouth breakwater and grounded. She was broken up at Newport in 1959.

HMS *Cornwall*

Completed in 1928 at Devonport Dockyard, the pre-war service of this Kent Class cruiser was on the China Station. During 1940 and 1941 she was posted to the South Atlantic and also patrolled the Indian Ocean. On 7 May 1941, north of the Seychelles, she sank the German raider *Pinguin*. On 5 April 1942 she was sunk by Japanese aircraft off Ceylon.

HMS *Dorsetshire*

Completed in 1930, this Norfolk Class cruiser served on the China, Africa and South Atlantic stations. Her most famous action during the Second World War was delivering the *coup de grâce* to the German battleship *Bismarck* in May 1941. After the *Bismarck* had been reduced to floating wreckage by Royal Navy battleships, cruisers, including the *Dorsetshire*, were sent in to finish her off. Two torpedoes fired by the *Dorsetshire* did the trick. In 1942 she joined the Eastern Fleet. Sailing on a patrol sweep in company with HMS *Cornwall* in the Indian Ocean, on 5 April of that year, she came under attack from Japanese aircraft and was sunk.

HMS *Devonshire*

A London Class cruiser completed at Devonport Dockyard in March 1929, after war service she was commissioned as a cadets' training ship from 1947 to 1953. She was broken up at Cashmores, Newport, in 1954.

HMS *Exeter*

After the battleship *Warspite*, HMS *Exeter* is perhaps Devonport's best-loved Second World War era warship. She is pictured here moving up river to Devonport Dockyard during the 1930s. Her exploits at the Battle of the River Plate in 1939 are well documented, as is her return to Devonport, where she received a joyous welcome from the people of Plymouth in celebration of the victory over the German pocket battleship *Graf Spee* on the Plate. After repairs and a refit she sailed for the Far East to joined the ABDA (American, British, Dutch and Australian) Command under Admiral Doorman. On 28 February 1942 she sailed in the company of HMS *Encounter* and USS *Pope* for Colombo. On the following morning she came under attack from Japanese cruisers. HMS *Exeter* and the two destroyers were sunk.

HMS *Kent*

Name ship of a cruiser class, she was launched at Chatham Dockyard in 1926. At the outbreak of the Second World War she and the French cruiser *Suffren* helped protect the East Indies from the threat of ocean raiders. In September 1940 she was torpedoed in the Mediterranean, suffering severe damage. In 1941, while in dock at Devonport for repairs, she was struck by a bomb and further damaged. After repairs she joined the Home Fleet at Scapa Flow. She helped escort eighteen convoys to Russia. Reduced to the Reserve after the war, she was then placed on the disposal list and arrived at Troon in January 1948 to be broken up.

HMS *Ranpura*

A former P & O liner requisitioned in 1940 for service as an armed merchant cruiser, during the Second World War she transported gold bullion from Plymouth to Canada and the United States to purchase war materiel. She was converted to a heavy repair ship in 1945 for service in the Mediterranean. Having been paid off into the Reserve, she was sold in April 1961 and arrived at Spezia in May 1961 to be broken up.

HMS *Norfolk*

Completed in May 1930, this Norfolk Class cruiser took part in many operations during the war, including helping to hunt down the *Bismarck*. She was also involved in the Battle of North Cape on Boxing Day 1943, in which the German battle cruiser *Scharnhorst* was sunk. HMS *Norfolk* was lucky to survive this clash, as one of the German warship's 11-inch shells hit her, but sliced through her without exploding. After the war she was placed in reserve and then sent to Newport in 1950 to be broken up.

HMS *Parthian*

Launched at Chatham Dockyard in June 1929, during the war she went to the Mediterranean. In August 1943 she was lost, presumed sunk by a mine in the southern Adriatic.

HMS *Ardent*

An 'A' Class destroyer built by Scotts and launched in June 1929, she took part in the 1933 Jubilee Fleet Review. In June 1940, in company with HMS *Acasta*, she was tasked with escorting the carrier HMS *Glorious* following the evacuation of British forces from Norway. The three British warships were found by the German battle cruiser *Scharnhorst* and cruiser *Gneisenau*. All the British ships were sunk. Only three sailors survived from *Ardent*'s crew.

HMS *Resource*

A fleet repair ship launched at Vickers Armstrong in November 1928, she was to serve with the Mediterranean and Eastern Fleets. After the war she was put in reserve until 1951, when she was placed in the sales list. She arrived at M/S Wards, Inverkeithing, to be broken up, in February 1954.

HMS *Kuroki*

Pictured here in Plymouth Sound in 1943 on boom defence duties, she is a good example of the many small ships that did mundane, but essential, work that was hardly noticed by the general public. Requisitioned by the Royal Navy in 1940, she was returned to her owners in 1946.

HMT *Northcoates*

A trawler built in 1919, she was requisitioned from J. Marr and Sons, Fleetwood, in 1939 for service as a minesweeper. August 1942 saw her join the Plymouth Command, where she remained until December of that year, when, due to stress of the weather, she sank while under tow by HMT *Resolve*. All her crew were saved.

HMS *Albatross*

Completed in 1928 at the Cockatoo Yard, Sydney, as a seaplane carrier/tender. She was transferred to the Royal Navy in 1938 and served until 1946, when she was sold to commercial interests and renamed *Pride of Torquay*.

HMS *Alaunia*

Built as a passenger liner for the Cunard Steamship Company in 1925, she was taken into naval service in 1939 and converted to an armed merchant cruiser. She was purchased by the Royal Navy and became a fleet heavy repair ship in 1944. In later years, as the fleet was run down, she became surplus and arrived at Blyth for breaking up in September 1957.

HMS *Penzance*

One of the many sloops built at Devonport Dockyard during the 1930s. Shortly before the start of the Second World War she sailed for the America, West Indies Station. In August 1940, while escorting Convoy SC1, she was sunk by *U37* in the North Atlantic.

HMS *Grimsby*

Another Devonport-built sloop. In 1934 her first commission took her to the Far East, where she remained until 1939. During 1940 she joined the Eastern Mediterranean Fleet. On 25 May 1941, while off Tobruk, she was attacked by enemy aircraft and sunk.

HMS *Fearless*

Completed in 1934 by Cammell Laird, on the outbreak of war she was serving with the 8th Destroyer Flotilla based at Scapa Flow. Her early Second World War service saw her in action off Norway and at Mers-El-Kebir during the British fleet's attack on Vichy French naval forces. On 23 July 1941 she was attacked by Italian aircraft while helping to escort a Malta convoy. Two torpedoes were dropped and one hit *Fearless*. A raging fire swept through her. Survivors were taken off and she was sunk – to prevent her falling into enemy hands – by HMS *Forester*.

HMS *Griffin*

A 'G' Class destroyer launched in 1935, she served in the Mediterranean until 1939, when she returned to home waters. She was later transferred to the Royal Canadian Navy and renamed HMCS *Ottawa*. In company with other British and Canadian warships she sank the Italian submarine *Lafole* in October 1940. She also claimed U*678* in July 1944, plus U*621* and U*984* in August of the same year. The start of 1945 saw her as a member of the 11th Escort Group, based at Londonderry. Twelve months later she was paid off for disposal in Nova Scotia.

HMS *Leith*

Launched in September 1933 at Devonport, her first commission took her to New Zealand waters, where she remained until she returned home in 1939. Her wartime service saw her employed on escort duties. After the war she was laid up until 1946, when she was sold to Panamanian owners. In 1948 she changed hands to become the *Friendship*, owned by the Danish World Friendship Association. In 1950 she was taken over by the Royal Danish Navy for deep-sea exploration and renamed *Galatea*. She was sold for breaking up in October 1955.

HMS *Ullswater*

A trawler, pictured here in Plymouth Sound in 1941, she had been completed in 1939. She was then requisitioned for naval service, operating out of Scapa Flow and Belfast and patrolling the Channel. On 19 November 1942, while escorting a convoy south of Plymouth, she came under attack and was sunk along with three freighters.

HMS *Wellington*

On completion in 1935 she commissioned for service on the New Zealand station. In 1937 she recommissioned at her name port, remaining there until 1939, when she was temporarily attached to the China Station. She later took part in Operation Cycle (the evacuation of British troops from France in June 1940), and the North African landings of 1942/43 and operated out of Gibraltar on escort duties. She was then employed on locating surrendered U-boats until August 1945, when she was laid up at Milford Haven. In June 1947 she was purchased by the Hon. Company of Master Mariners for use as their London headquarters, a function she performs to this day, moored on the Thames.

HMS *Fowey*

Another sloop built at Devonport and completed in 1931, her war service included the sinking of U*55* off Ushant in company with HMS *Whitshed*. After the war she was sold to Chinese owners and left Falmouth in 1947 for Shanghai. After a short life in her new role she was scrapped at Mombasa in 1950.

HMS *Leander*

On completion in 1933 she became flagship of the 2nd Cruiser Squadron. She was the first Royal Navy cruiser with a single funnel. After war service she was paid off into reserve at Devonport in 1948 and then, in January 1950, was sent for breaking up at Blyth.

HMS *Ajax*

This cruiser's battle honours speak for themselves: River Plate, 1939; Mediterranean, 1940–41; Matapan, 1941; Greece, 1941; Crete, 1941; Malta Convoys, 1941; Aegean, 1941; Normandy, 1944; South of France, 1944. Laid up at Falmouth in 1948, she was broken up at Cashmores, Newport in 1949.

HMS *Defender*

Commissioned in 1932, this destroyer spent her pre-war service on the Mediterranean, China and Red Sea stations. In 1940 she joined the fleet in the Mediterranean and survived many hazardous operations until 11 July 1941, when she came under air attack off Tobruk and a near miss broke her back. She was taken under tow by HMAS *Vendetta* but seven miles from Sidi Barani it became clear she was hopeless case, so her crew were taken off and (as shown here) she was sunk by *Vendetta*.

HMS *Orion*

A Leander Class cruiser built at Devonport and completed in 1933, she played a prominent part in operations in the Mediterranean during the war, sustaining serious damage during the evacuation of British and Dominion troops from Crete in May 1941. She was sold in 1949 and broken up at Troon.

HMS *Grafton*

Completed by Thornycroft in 1936, *Grafton* had a short life as, on 29 May 1940, she was torpedoed off Dunkirk while taking part in the evacuation of British and French troops.

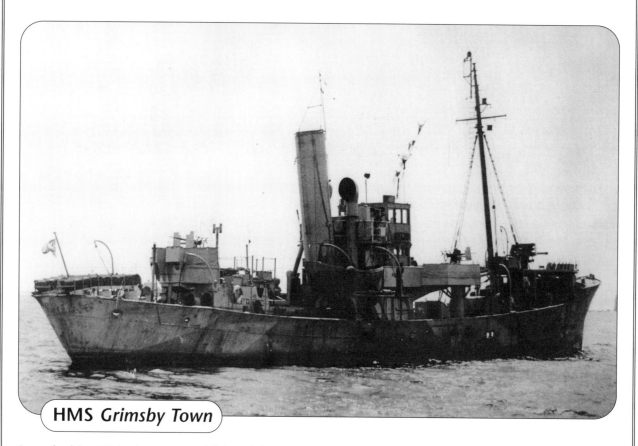

HMS *Grimsby Town*

Launched in 1934, she was requisitioned for naval service in August 1939. She is pictured here serving as an anti-submarine patrol vessel in 1943. She was returned to her owners in November 1945.

HMS *Thames*

HMS *Thames* was to meet a mysterious end in the Second World War. She left for a patrol in July 1940, heading for waters off Norway, and never returned. It is believed she hit mines in the North Sea during her passage to the patrol area. HMS *Thames* was one of three large River Class boats built in the 1930s. These swift submarines were meant to ride with surface ship task groups to protect them and to act as pickets far out in front to detect any approaching aggressors.

HMS *Inglefield*

On joining the command of C-in-C Western Approaches in 1939, her first duty was to escort the carrier HMS *Courageous*. During that duty she was sent to the aid of a merchant ship that had been torpedoed. While she was away HMS *Courageous* was sunk. In February 1944, while off the Anzio beachhead in Italy, she came under attack from aircraft and was sunk by a German glider bomb.

HMS *Garland*

Launched in October 1935 by Fairfields, she was transferred to the Polish Navy in May 1940 and served in many theatres of war. After her return to the Royal Navy she was transferred again in 1947, this time to the Royal Netherlands Navy, and renamed *Marnix*.

HMS *Auckland*

Built by Dennys in 1938, HMS *Auckland* was one of three sloops of the Egret Class, and was originally to be named *Heron*. But, as she was assigned to the Royal New Zealand Navy, she was renamed *Auckland*. In April 1940 she took part in combined operations off Norway and was damaged by aircraft off Namsos. On completion of repairs she sailed for the Mediterranean, where she took part in the evacuation of Greece and the Battle of Crete. In June 1941, while off Tobruk she was attacked by Italian aircraft and sunk. The three pictures here show her being bombed and sinking.

HMS *Gloucester*

Name ship of a cruiser class, she was launched at Devonport in 1937. On completion she sailed for the Mediterranean, then went to the East Indies as a flagship. During 1940 she returned to the Med and took part in Malta Convoys, the Battle of Matapan and attacks on enemy shipping. In May 1941, while off Crete, she was bombed by German and Italian aircraft and sunk, with heavy loss of life.

HMS *Penelope*

Built by Harland and Wolff, she was one of four ships of the Arethusa Class of cruisers. Much of her wartime service was in the Mediterranean, where she earned the nickname HMS *Pepperpot*, due to the number of patches covering the damage she had received. On 11 February 1944, while off Anzio, she was torpedoed by U*410* and sank.

HMS *Birmingham*

Built at Devonport, war service took this Southampton Class cruiser to many parts of the world. In June 1942 she was damaged by enemy air attack during a Malta convoy run. On passage through the Mediterranean in 1943 she was torpedoed by U407 and suffered severe damage. She survived to take part in the Korean War of the early 1950s and became Flagship, Second-in-Command Far East. On return to home waters she was placed in reserve, then sold for breaking up, arriving at Wards, Inverkeithing, in September 1960.

HMS *Belfast*

Commissioned in 1939, her active service life was to be delayed, as she struck a mine in the Firth of Forth and broke her back. She was towed to Devonport, repaired and returned to service in 1942. She formed part of the force that sank the *Scharnhorst* in December 1943 at the Battle of North Cape. After the war she was modernized and served in the Far East. On her return to Devonport she underwent a repair programme and, on completion, was placed in reserve. She then went to Portsmouth to act as Reserve Fleet HQ until 1970. In 1971 she became a museum ship in the Pool of London, which is where she is to this day.

HMS *Edinburgh*

The *Edinburgh* was not to be as lucky as her sister ship, HMS *Belfast*. Pictured here in Plymouth Sound, she was launched in March 1938. During the years 1939 to 1942 she served with the Home Fleet. In 1942, while in the Barents Sea off Russia, she was torpedoed by *U456*, then attacked by three German destroyers. She managed to sink one of them, but was hit by another torpedo. Her bows and her stern had been blown off, but still she remained afloat. At the time she was carrying Russian bullion – the so-called 'Stalin's Gold' – which was intended to pay for arms shipments from the Allies to the Soviets. *Edinburgh* was dead in the water and, with marauding Germans all around, it was thought best to scuttle her. The gold was recovered by a salvage team nearly fifty years later.

HMS *Tartar*

A member of the famous Tribal Class of destroyers that took part in so many Second World War actions, *Tartar* was one of only four ships of the 16-strong class to survive the war. In August 1942 HMS *Tartar* was one of 12 escorting destroyers in the Mediterranean protecting the Pedestal Convoy to Malta, which took place at the height of the Axis siege of the strategically vital island. On 13 August she had to sink the destroyer *Foresight*, which had been torpedoed and crippled by an Italian torpedo bomber the previous day. The next month she was in the Arctic, riding shotgun on the PQ18 convoy to Murmansk. During 1944 she helped sink several German destroyers. By the end of the war HMS *Tartar* was in action against the Japanese with the East Indies Fleet. Placed in reserve in 1946, she arrived at Cashmores, Newport, in January 1948 to be broken up.

Canadian Flotilla at Plymouth

The *Huron*, a sister ship of the *Athabaskan* (see below), was launched in June 1942, having been built by Swan Hunter on the Tyne. She saw action throughout the Second World War with the Royal Canadian Navy. She was eventually withdrawn from service and sold to breakers at Spezia in August 1965.

HMCS *Huron*

HMCS *Athabaskan*

Launched in 1941, this Canadian destroyer was based in Plymouth during the Second World War. On 29 April 1944, in an action with German torpedo boats off the French Coast, she was hit by a torpedo and blew up.

Now preserved in Canada as a memorial, she, like her sisters, was based at Plymouth. She was to see further service in the Korean War. After withdrawal from the fleet, in August 1964 she was offered to the City of Toronto as a memorial to Canadian sailors in the Second World War. Well preserved, she is now the focal point of the Haida Association.

HMCS *Haida*

HMS *Ellesmere*

A Lake Class trawler built by Smiths Dock and launched in 1939. The six ships of the class were purchased by the Royal Navy for war service. While on patrol in the Channel in February 1945 HMS *Ellesmere* was torpedoed and sunk.

HMS *Cleveland*

Completed in 1940, she was a Hunt Class destroyer that took part in the St Nazaire commando raid, in March 1942, and supported the landings at Salerno, in 1943, and the South of France, in 1944. Paid off into the reserve, she was sold in June 1957 and while en route to the breakers ran aground on Rhossili Sands. After stripping, her hulk was blown up in December 1959.

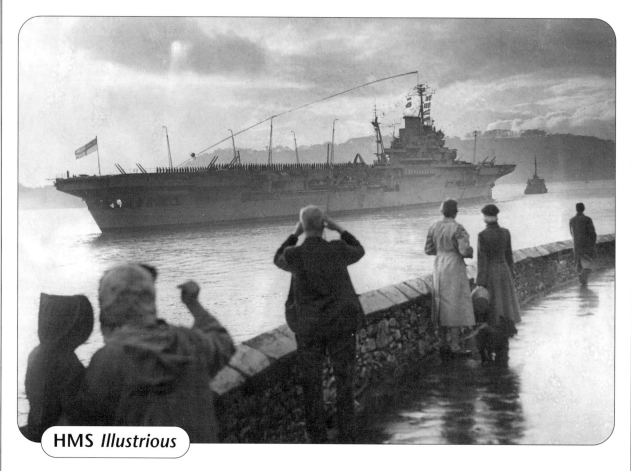

HMS *Illustrious*

A fleet carrier that became famous during the Second World War, as she was the launch pad for the Swordfish torpedo bomber attack on the Italian fleet at Taranto in November 1940 in which three battleships were put out of action. It inspired the Japanese to devise a similar plan to strike a blow at the US Navy in port at Pearl Harbor thirteen months later. She also did sterling service on the extremely hazardous Malta Convoys. *Illustrious* is pictured here flying her paying-off pennant as she makes her way up river to Devonport Dockyard. Her postwar career was one of trials and training until 1954, when she was placed in reserve and then handed over to the British Iron and Steel Corporation to be broken up at Faslane.

HMS *Junon*

A French Diane Class submarine, on the fall of France she was taken under Royal Navy control. During the war she ran into the problem of spares and spent many months out of service. Placed in reserve in December 1944, she was ultimately returned to the French Navy. She then served as a training ship until 1950.

HMS *Adamant*

A submarine depot ship completed in 1942 by Harland and Wolff, Belfast, she served in many theatres of war. From 1948 to 1953 she was Senior Officer's Ship Reserve Fleet, Portsmouth. She then went to Faslane, where she remained until 1963, as the 3rd Submarine Squadron Depot Ship. Her last commission was at Devonport with the 2nd Submarine Squadron, again as depot ship, until paid off and replaced by HMS *Forth*. She arrived at Inverkeithing in September 1970 to be broken up.

HMS *Bulolo*

Taken into naval service early in the war, she was converted to an armed merchant cruiser. In 1942 she again underwent conversion, to a landing ship headquarters. She then took part in many amphibious assault operations and remained in naval service until December 1946, when she was handed back to her owners.

HMS *Implacable*

An Implacable Class fleet carrier launched in 1942, she served with the Home and Pacific fleets. As the war clouds gathered over Europe in 1937, the rearming of Britain's armed forces was finally well under way, with the Royal Navy getting modern aircraft carriers. By the time war broke out in September 1939 three new classes of aircraft carrier, Illustrious, Indomitable and Implacable, had been ordered. The decision to build these aircraft carriers with armoured flight-decks was a wise one. When under attack from kamikaze aircraft off Japan in the closing stages of the war British aircraft carriers like *Implacable* could weather a hit, while the American carriers (with unarmoured decks) were put out of action. In 1949, after coming through the final phase of the war unscathed, she became Flagship C-in-C Home Fleet. In 1954 she was reduced to the Reserve, then sold and broken up at Inverkeithing, arriving there in November 1955.

HMS *Switha*

An Isle Class trawler that performed a variety of duties during the war years, in 1946 she became a wreck dispersal vessel working in the Thames Estuary. In 1950 she became a tank cleaning vessel based at Devonport.

HMT *Plugastel*

A French Navy harbour tug seized for British service on 3 July 1940 while berthed at Plymouth, she served with the Royal Navy from 1940 to 1945 on minewatching duties. She was returned to French Navy in June 1945.

HMS *Thistle*

A 'T' Class submarine (First Group), the war had commenced by the time *Thistle* entered service and she was immediately ordered to help escort troop ships operating off the Norwegian coast. On 10 April 1940 she was torpedoed by *U4* and lost.

HMS *Trinidad*

Built by Devonport Dockyard and completed in 1941, in March 1942, while on Russian convoy duties, this Fiji Class cruiser engaged three German destroyers, firing torpedoes at them. However, one of her own turned and hit her. She was towed to Murmansk in Russia's Kola Inlet for temporary repairs. She sailed for the UK after this work was completed but came under attack again, this time from torpedo-carrying aircraft of the Luftwaffe. She was hit and then abandoned, but stayed afloat. She had to be sunk by HMS *Matchless* on 15 May 1942. She is known in Royal Navy folklore as 'The Ship that Torpedoed Herself'.

HMS *Torbay*

Launched in 1940, she had a short but active life, during which her captain won the Victoria Cross for his action against enemy shipping in Corfu Roads in 1942. She also served in the Far East and frequently patrolled the dangerous Malacca Straits searching for Japanese prey. On her return home she was paid off and sent to be broken up by M/S Wards at Briton Ferry.

HMS *Ulysses*

A wartime destroyer that served as a stopgap anti-submarine frigate until new constructions came into service (she was converted to a Type 15 frigate in 1952–3). Sold off in 1979, she was broken up by M/S Davies and Cann at Plymouth. She is pictured here arriving at Devonport to be paid off.

HMS *Newcastle*

Completed in 1937, she served in the Atlantic and South Atlantic and with the Eastern Fleet/East Indies Fleet. During the Plymouth Blitz of 1941 she was caught in the middle of falling bombs while under repair at Devonport. Her guns were used in the defence of the city. After the war she underwent reconstruction and sailed for service in the Far East. Towards the end of the 1950s she was paid off. She arrived at Shipbreaking Industries, Faslane, in August 1959 to be broken up.

HMS *Clematis*

Built at Bristol and completed in 1940, HMS *Clematis* was a Flower Class corvette and spent spent most of her war on convoy escort duties, but in 1944 she supported the Normandy landings. Paid off in June 1945, she was sold for scrap in 1949 and broken up at Charlestown.

HMS *Black Swan*

Name ship of a class of frigates, she saw a lot of action in the Second World War. Damaged twice by German aircraft, she got her revenge in helping to sink U*124*. After the Second World War she was to grab headlines in the early Cold War era, making a name for herself in the Yangtze Incident of 1949, during which she ran a gauntlet of Communist guns down the Chinese river. During the Korean War, in company with the cruiser HMS *Jamaica*, she took part in the first naval action of the conflict. The two warships sank six North Korean E-Boats. She returned to Devonport in November 1951 and was placed in the Reserve. She was sent to Troon in 1956 to be broken up.

HMS *Britomart*

A Halcyon Class minesweeper built at Devonport and commissioned in 1939, in August 1944, while operating off the coast of Normandy, she and HMS *Hussar* were mistaken for enemy vessels by RAF fighter-bombers and attacked. Twenty-two of the *Britomart*'s crew were killed and she sank. HMS *Hussar* was also sunk.

HMS *Tyne*

A depot ship launched in 1940, after her war service she was laid up at Harwich from 1946 to 1948. She then went to the Mediterranean and Far East for service before returning home in 1955. She was used as an accommodation ship at Portsmouth before being towed to Devonport to become Headquarters Ship, Reserve Fleet Maintenance. She remained there until 1972, when she was sold off and sent for breaking up at Barrow. She is pictured here with HMS *Badsworth* and HMS *Lively* berthed alongside in Iceland, which was an Royal Navy operating base in the Second World War, in August 1941.

HMS *Bermuda*

A Fiji Class cruiser, pictured here at anchor in Plymouth Sound, under Staddon Heights. Note the Sunderland aircraft that has just taken off from RAF Mount Batten behind her. Her wartime and peace-time service was to take her to the four corners of the world. As the navy was run down after the war so the requirement for large crewed ships was reduced. Paid off in 1962, she was sold and arrived at M/S T.W. Ward, Briton Ferry, in August 1965 to be broken up.

HMS *Mauritius*

Launched in 1939, she was another Fiji Class cruiser. Pictured here in Plymouth Sound, with Fort Bovisand in the background, she was completed in 1941. She served on the Home, Mediterranean, Eastern and South Atlantic stations until 1953, when she was placed in reserve, then put on the disposal list in 1960. She arrived at M/S Wards, Inverkeithing, in March 1965 to be broken up.

HMS *Roberts*

Pictured here in 1946 at the North Yard, Devonport, this venerable monitor used her big gun fire-power – she was the last Royal Navy warship to mount 15-inch guns – to support the Normandy and Walcheren landings during the Second World War. After the war she was used in a variety of roles for twenty years. She left Plymouth for the last time in July 1965, bound for the breaker's yard at Inverkeithing.

HMS *Petard*

One of the wartime 'P' Class destroyers, after a distinguished Second World War career she underwent a limited conversion, then joined the Reserve Fleet at Devonport, lying in the No. 5 Basin for many years. As the Navy was run down and new constructions joined the fleet, she was paid off and sold to P. & W. McClelland, Bo'ness, arriving there in 1967.

HMS *Milne*

An 'M' Class destroyer launched in December 1941, her wartime service saw her take part in Operation Torch and sink U*289* off Norway, and she was also part of the force that tried to attack the *Tirpitz* in the Altenfjord in 1944. She was sold to Turkey in 1957 and renamed *Alp Arslam*. She was placed on the disposal list by her Turkish owners in August 1971.

HMS *Charybidis*

Completed in December 1941, her battle honours show this Dido Class cruiser had an a hectic service life: Malta Convoys, 1942; North Africa, 1942; Salerno, 1943; Atlantic, 1943; English Channel, 1943; Biscay, 1943. She was attacked off the northern coast of France by German torpedo boats on 23 October 1943 and sunk with the loss of 462 officers and men.

HMS *Loyal*

Launched on 8 October 1941, she hit a mine off the coast of Italy on 12 October 1944 and became a constructive loss. She was then used as a base ship at Malta until February 1948, when she was towed to M/S T.W. Ward, Milford Haven, and broken up.

HMS *Stanley*

Formerly the USS *McCalla*, she was one of the fifty destroyers transferred to the Royal Navy by the USA. She is pictured here undergoing reconstruction in Devonport to a long-range escort. *Stanley* was lost off Portugal in December 1941 after being torpedoed by *U574*.

HMS *Lookout*

Launched by Scotts in November 1940, after wartime service she was placed in reserve until 1948, when she was towed to Cashmores of Newport and broken up.

HMS *Thorn*

A 'T' Class submarine launched by Cammell Laird in March 1941. On completion HMS *Thorn* went to the Mediterranean, where, in August 1942, during an attack against enemy shipping off Crete she was sunk by the Italian torpedo boat *Pegaso*.

HMS *Eclipse*

This destroyer was in the thick of it from the start of the Second World War, being damaged off Norway in 1940. After repairs she went to Scapa Flow. In 1942 she escorted many convoys to Russia and in April 1943 she was loaned to Western Approaches Command. She then went to the Mediterranean, where she took part in the Sicily landings. She also supported the landings at Salerno, during which, in company with HMS *Laforey*, she brought the Italian submarine *Ascianghi* to the surface and sank her by gunfire. On 23 October 1943, while off Kalimno, with 200 troops onboard, she hit a mine and sank. Survivors were picked up by HMS *Petard*.

HMS *Kujawiak*

Launched in 1940 as the Hunt Class destroyer HMS *Oakley*, she was handed over to the Polish Navy before completion and renamed. In December 1941 she was part of the force that landed commandos on the Lofoten Islands. In March 1942 she was damaged and suffered casualties from air attack. In June 1942, while escorting a convoy to Malta she was attacked by aircraft, submarines and surface vessels, but survived. On 15 June she was mined off Malta and sank under tow the next day.

HMS *Malcolm*

Completed in 1919, during the Second World War she took part in the Dunkirk evacuation of May 1940 and by 1942 had been converted to a short-range escort. During convoy duties she helped sink the *U651* off Iceland and took part in Malta and Russian convoys. She was then paid off, sold to T.W. Ward and arrived at Barrow on 25 July 1945 to be broken up.

HMS *Pathfinder*

Launched in April 1941, her wartime service saw her help sink the Italian submarine *Cobalto* and the German U*162*. She later helped sink U*203*. HMS *Pathfinder* ended her war with the East Indies Fleet in the Far East, where, in February 1945, she was bombed by Japanese aircraft and badly damaged. She was towed back to Britain and used as a floating air target until sold to M/S Howells and scrapped at Falmouth in November 1948.

HMS *Termagant*

Completed in December 1943, her wartime service took her from Arctic convoys to the British Pacific Fleet. In 1952–3 she underwent a limited conversion to an anti-submarine frigate. Paid off, she was sold to Arnott Young and arrived at Dalmuir on 5 November 1965 to be broken up.

HMS *Caesar*

Completed in February 1944, she was one of the last destroyers to mount single guns as main arma-
ment. From 1957 to 1960 she underwent a refit at Rosyth before being commissioned as Leader of the
8th Destroyer Squadron.

Caesar was one of four ships in the eight-strong class to be given an enclosed bridge during refitting,
which enabled her to operate in the nuclear–biological warfare environment of the Cold War. From 1960
to 1965 she served in the Far East and saw further service with the 24th and 26th Escort Squadrons
before being paid off at Chatham. In January 1967 she arrived at Blyth to be broken up.

Devonport Dockyard

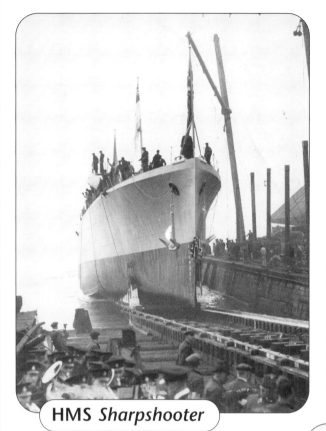

HMS *Sharpshooter*

Pictured here is the launch of HMS *Sharpshooter* at Devonport Dockyard in 1936. After war service HMS *Sharpshooter* was commissioned as a survey vessel. In 1953 she was renamed *Shackleton* and surveyed waters off the West of England, in the Bristol Channel and the Irish Sea. Paid off in November 1962, she was placed in reserve, then sold to the West of Scotland Shipbreaking Company, arriving at Troon in November 1965 to be broken up.

It is July 1943, and we see HMS *Starling* in dry dock at the Keyham Yard, Devonport, for repairs to her forefoot or stem.

HMS *Starling*

HMS *Terrible*

HMS *Terrible* was the only aircraft carrier to be built at Devonport Royal Dockyard. Launched in September 1944, she is pictured here on the stocks in the dockyard and also moving into Plymouth Sound. She was handed over to the Royal Australian Navy in December 1948 and renamed HMAS *Sydney*. She later took part in the Korean War, sailed in the 1953 Coronation Review and was converted to a training ship, finally paying off in 1958. In 1961–2 she underwent conversion to a fast troop vessel, then reverted to being a training ship. In 1973 she was withdrawn from service and then sold off for scrap, arriving in South Korea in December 1975 to be broken up.

HMS *Brocklesby*

Launched in September 1940, after war service this escort destroyer had a varied career: aircraft target training, Asdic training and service with the 2nd Frigate Squadron. Paid off in June 1963, she arrived at Faslane in October 1968 to be broken up.

HMS *Tigris*

Launched in October 1939, HMS *Tigris* was lost (cause unknown) in the Bay of Naples in March 1943.

HMS *United*

Formerly the *P44*, HMS *United* was launched in December 1941. After serving in the war she was placed in reserve. Paid off, she was sold in February 1946 and broken up at Troon.

HMS *Black Prince*

A Dido Class cruiser launched in 1942, after the war she was loaned to the Royal New Zealand Navy, then placed in reserve until 1952. Recommissioned, she took part in the Coronation Review of 1953 and then went home and into reserve again until 1962, when she was sold off and broken up in Japan.

HMS *Orwell*

One of the first emergency destroyers built under the war programme, she was launched in April 1942. She is pictured here in October 1942, just after completion. After war service she spent many years in reserve before undergoing conversion to a Type 16 frigate. She operated from Rosyth, Devonport and Portsmouth before being sold for scrap and sent to Cashmores, Newport, to be broken up.

HMS *Stonehenge*

An 'S' Class submarine launched in 1943. November 1944 saw her leave the United Kingdom for Trincomalee to patrol off the Nicobar Islands. Nothing more was heard from her and she was presumed lost and paid off.

HMT *Bervie Braes*

Requisitioned by the Royal Navy and used on patrol and minesweeping duties, she was returned to her owners in October 1944. The main reason why this photograph has been included is the large amount of interesting background detail it contains, such as the anti-submarine boom defence gates in Plymouth Sound which needed vessels to open and close them. The photograph was taken in 1943.

HMS *Icarus*

Launched in November 1936, wartime service of this 'I' Class destroyer saw her sink the U*45* and U*35* in 1939. Early in 1940 she laid mines off Norway and was present at the Second Battle of Narvik. She later sustained damage while being attacked by enemy aircraft, but she was still able to take part in the hunt for the *Bismarck* in May 1941. She later escorted Russian convoys and in March 1944 helped sink U*744* off Ireland after a long hunt. In January 1945 she also helped sink U*1199* off Land's End. She was paid off and broken up at Troon in October 1946.

HMS *Mahratta*

An 'M' Class destroyer launched in July 1942, she was originally to be called *Marksman*. Her launch was delayed as she was blown off the stocks during an air raid on the Clyde. While off northern Norway on 25 February 1944 she was torpedoed by *U990* and sank, and only seventeen of her crew survived.

HMS *Flamingo*

Launched in April 1939, she was a Black Swan Class sloop. After war service she was refitted at Devonport, then went to the Persian Gulf, where she remained from 1946 to 1956, except for refits. Placed in reserve in 1956, she was sold to West Germany and renamed *Graf Spee*. She was broken up in 1965.

HMS *Limbourne*

Completed in 1942, she joined the 15th Destroyer Flotilla based at Plymouth in December of that year. During 1943 she carried out many operational tasks, including escort duties, anti-submarine sweeps and protection duties. During Operation Tunnel in October 1943 – an offensive sweep off the north coast of Brittany – she came under attack from E-boats and was struck by a torpedo. Attempts were made to take her in tow and bring her home, but bad weather forced her to be scuttled.

HMS *Howe*

The Royal Navy's four King George V battleships – HMS *Howe*, HMS *Prince of Wales*, HMS *Duke of York* and HMS *Anson* – were ordered under the 1936 naval building programme. All ships of this class were laid down in 1937, but owing to competition for limited ship-building resources during the final run-up to hostilities and the early part of the war itself, it took until August 1942 to complete HMS *Howe*. She was built by Fairfield and had been launched in April 1940. Her service in the Second World War included participating in the final sea campaign against the Japanese in the Pacific. In 1946 she became a training ship, later serving as Headquarters ship of the Reserve Fleet at Portsmouth. She was then laid up at Devonport in mothballs before being sold off for breaking up in 1958.

HMS *Anson*

Completed in June 1942, this King George V Class battleship first saw service on the Russian convoys runs and patrols off the Norwegian coast. She then went to the Mediterranean before sailing for the Far East. She was a member of the force that relieved Hong Kong after the Japanese surrender and was later a guardship at Tokyo. On return to the UK she joined a training squadron until she was paid off. She was then sold and arrived at Faslane in December 1957 to be broken up.

HMS *Jervis*

Pictured here in June 1945, this 'J' Class destroyer was launched in September 1938. Her wartime service saw her take part in the Battle of Matapan, where, together with the destroyer HMS *Nubian*, she sank the Italian cruiser *Pola*. She was also present at the evacuation of Crete and supported the Normandy landings. After the war she was paid off for disposal and arrived at Port Banatyne in January 1949 to be broken up by M/S Arnott Young.

HMS *Newport*

A destroyer transferred to the Royal Navy in 1940 by the US Navy, she arrived at Devonport to be refitted. On completion she was loaned to the Royal Norwegian Navy. In 1942 she collided with the destroyer HMS *Beverley*. She was returned to the Royal Navy before the completion of repairs. She later became an air target ship. Paid off in July 1945, she was then handed to M/S Brechin and arrived at Granton on 18 February 1947 to be broken up.

HMS *Spartan*

Launched in August 1942 and completed in August 1943, the Bellona Class cruiser HMS *Spartan* served with the Home and Mediterranean fleets. On 29 January 1944, while off Anzio, she capsized after being hit by a glider bomb.

HMS *Royalist*

Completed in September 1943, the wartime service of this Bellona Class cruiser took her on Arctic patrols and operations in support of the Normandy landings and later to the Mediterranean. In company with HMS *Teazer*, in September 1944 she sank two German ships in the Aegean Sea. She also went to the Far East, giving gunfire support for the capture of Rangoon in 1945. She was modernized at Devonport from 1954 to 1956, and then served with the Royal New Zealand Navy until she was paid off and broken up in Japan in 1968.

HMS *Roebuck*

This destroyer had the distinction of being 'launched' by a near miss during an air raid on Greenock, when the blast sent her down the slipway. After war service in the Far East she underwent conversion to an anti-submarine frigate and became a familiar sight in Plymouth Sound. Paid off in 1968, she was used for underwater explosions trials before being sold to M/S T.W. Ward and broken up at Inverkeithing in June 1968.

HMS *Modeste*

Completed in September 1945, she was placed in reserve in Devonport until February 1946, when she became a gunnery training ship at Portsmouth. She then saw service in the Mediterranean and the Suez invasion of 1956 before returning to the UK. She was then paid off and placed in reserve at Devonport again. Sold to M/S T.A. White, she arrived at St David's in March 1961 to be broken up.

HMS *Tavy*

Built by Chas Hill at Bristol and launched in 1943, after the war she was placed in reserve at Dartmouth, then Devonport, before going to Barrow-in-Furness. Having been paid off, she was sold to Cashmores and arrived at Newport to be broken up in 1955.

HMS *Hart*

Launched in 1943, she was later to take part in the Korean War then reduced to the Reserve in 1952. She arrived at Devonport in 1955 for refitting, after which she was sold to the West German Navy and renamed *Scheer* in 1958. She was paid off in 1968 and sold for breaking up in 1969.

HMS *Tally Ho*

A 'T' Class submarine launched in December 1942, she is pictured here in Plymouth Sound just after completion. Note the absence of boom defence nets. In the background of the photograph are a barrage balloon vessel and a Flower Class corvette. *Tally Ho*'s last duties for the Royal Navy were as a static training ship. Then she was paid off and sold to T.W. Ward, and arrived at Briton Ferry, Wales, in February 1967 to be broken up.

HMS *Mermaid*

Launched in November 1943, *Mermaid* was another sloop that ended her days with the West German Navy. She was transferred in May 1959 and renamed *Scharnhorst*.

HMS *Teme*

A River Class frigate launched in November 1943, HMS *Teme* was manned by the Royal Canadian Navy from 1944 until she was torpedoed by U*246* off Falmouth on 29 March 1945, suffering substantial damage. She was broken up by M/S Rees at Llanelli, arriving there on 8 December 1945.

HMS *Loch Fyne*

Completed in November 1944, her first commission the following year took her to the East Indies. She returned home in June 1946 and was placed in reserve. In October 1950 she was refitted for service with the 6th Frigate Flotilla, Home Fleet. April 1951 saw her take part in the search for the submarine *Affray*, which disappeared in deep waters off the Channel Islands. She arrived at Devonport in February 1955 and in June of that year she left for Southampton to be fitted for service in a tropical climate. For the next eight years, except for refits, she was stationed in the Persian Gulf. She arrived back at Devonport in May 1963 and was paid off for disposal. She arrived at Cashmores in August 1970 to be broken up.

HMS *St Austell Bay*

Launched in November 1944 and renamed, this Bay Class frigate was formerly named *Loch Lyddoch*, and was completed in May 1945. From 1945 to 1950 she served in the Mediterranean, then with the Home Fleet from 1951 to 1952. She then went to the America, West Indies Station for two years before returning to Devonport for a refit in September 1956. She was then placed in reserve, sold and arrived at Charlestown to be broken up by Shipbreaking Industries Ltd in July 1959.

HMS *Camperdown*

Launched in February 1944, this Battle Class destroyer is pictured here soon after completion (in June 1945). She then joined the British Pacific Fleet, returning home in early 1947 to be placed in reserve, where she remained for ten years. After a refit she replaced HMS *St Kitts* in the Mediterranean. She returned to Devonport and joined the Reserve Fleet, where she remained until sold, arriving at Faslane to be broken up in 1970.

HMS *Veryan Bay*

Built by Chas Hill and Sons, Bristol, and launched in November 1944, on completion she went to the Far East, then the Mediterranean and the West Indies. After refitting she spent more of her service on the America, West Indies Station until March 1957, when she arrived at Devonport to be paid off into the reserve. She was then sold and arrived at Charlestown to be broken up by Shipbreaking Industries Ltd in 1959.

HMS *Ocean*

A light fleet carrier completed in 1945, the first jet aircraft landing trials were carried out aboard her in December of the same year by a Sea Vampire. She later took part in the Korean War, flying off piston-powered Sea Fury fighters, which still managed to notch up kills against Mig jet fighters. She also played a leading role as a launch pad for Royal Marines commandos taking part in the ill-fated Suez Invasion of 1956. Placed in reserve in 1958, she was sold and broken up at Faslane in 1962. A new helicopter/commando carrier called HMS *Ocean* has now been built for the Royal Navy and is being based at Devonport Naval Base.

HMS *Loch Gorm*

The first commission of this Loch Class frigate was to the East Indies in 1945. She returned in 1946 and was placed in reserve at Devonport. In 1948 she had a refit and was placed in reserve again, this time at Barrow. She was later sold to the Kavounides Shipping Company of Greece and renamed *Orion*. She was broken up in Yugoslavia in 1966.

HMS *Loch Insh*

Another Loch Class frigate, *Loch Insh* was to spend many years on the East Indies/Persian Gulf Station, returning to Devonport for the last time in June 1962. In November 1963 she was refitted and then transferred to Malaya, renamed *Hang Tauh* and used as a training ship. She was withdrawn from service in 1977 and broken up.

HMS *Hogue*

A Battle Class destroyer launched in April 1944, she later joined the British Pacific Fleet but was withdrawn in 1947 and placed in reserve. She did not recommission for 10 years, until she joined the 1st Destroyer Squadron of the Mediterranean Fleet. Then, in 1959, she went to the Far East. On 25 August 1959 she collided with the Indian Navy cruiser *Mysore* and was badly damaged. She was broken up at Singapore in 1962.

HMS *Onyx*

Completed in March 1943, in 1945 she was at Hamburg and Cuxhaven on minesweeping duties and, after a refit at Liverpool, she joined the 18th Minesweeping Flotilla. She then went to the 3rd MSF at Port Edgar for six months before returning to Portsmouth in August 1947 and being laid up in reserve. In 1956 she returned to Devonport reserve, where she remained until sold in 1967 to be broken up at Inverkeithing.

HMS *Cockatrice*

An Algerine Class minesweeper launched in October 1942, she served with the Plymouth Command and the 18th Minesweeping Flotilla until August 1947. She then went to Rosyth and Harwich until placed in reserve at Chatham until August 1963, when she was sold to be broken up at Inverkeithing.

HMS *Fantome*

Launched in September 1942, she was mined off North Africa in May 1943. She managed to return to Devonport but was found to be a total constructive loss and paid off. She was sold to Wards and arrived at Milford Haven in May 1947 to be broken up.

HMS *Ready*

Launched in May 1943 by Harland and Wolff, Belfast, early 1945 saw her off the Dutch and Belgian coasts. Then, in August of that year, she started to sweep around the UK coastline. The following year saw her with Plymouth Command, then in 1948 she was placed in reserve. In 1951 she underwent a refit at Cowes. She was then sold to Belgium and renamed *Jan Van Haverbeke*. She was broken up in Belgium in 1961.

HMS *Opossum*

Completed in June 1945, this modified Black Swan Class sloop is pictured here on completion. Because the Royal Navy was being run down, like many ships she was placed in reserve almost immediately after the war. After a short refit in early 1952 she went to the Far East until 1958, when she returned to Devonport and was once more placed in reserve. She was sold in April 1960 to Demmelweek and Redding Ltd and broken up in Sutton Pool, Plymouth.

HMS *Oakham Castle*

A Castle Class corvette completed in December 1944, she was to spend long periods in dockyard hands undergoing modification. From 1948 to 1950 she served with the 2nd Training Squadron at Portland. In July 1957 she was transferred to the Air Ministry and renamed *Weather Reporter*. She was later withdrawn and arrived at Middlesbrough in November 1977 to be broken up.

HMS *Pheasant*

After war service this sloop was to spend many years in refit and reserve at Portsmouth, Barry and Devonport. In January 1963 while in tow from Devonport to Troon, where she was to be broken up, she broke away from the tug *Warden* off the north Cornish coast. The tow was later reconnected.

HMS *Bigbury Bay*

Named after a bay in South Devon not far from Plymouth, from completion in 1945 until 1958 she served on a variety of stations. In November 1958 she was reduced to the Reserve, then sold, in May 1959, to Portugal and renamed *Pacheco Pereira*. She was finally sold in 1970 for breaking up.

HMS *St Brides Bay*

Completed in June 1945, she was to spend four years in the Mediterranean before going to the Far East, where she spent a further 12 years. On return to the UK in December 1961 she was sold and arrived at Faslane in September 1962 to be broken up by Shipbreaking Industries Ltd.

HMS *Tremadoc Bay*

Built by Harland and Wolff, Belfast, and completed in October 1945, she served with the Devonport Local Flotilla from 1945 to 1951, when she was placed in reserve. In 1952 she went to Falmouth for refitting, returned to Devonport in 1953 and was placed in reserve. Later that year she was towed to Gibraltar to join the Reserve there. She was sent to Genoa in September 1959 to be broken up.

HMS *Cawsand Bay*

Like HMS *Bigbury Bay*, named after a bay near Plymouth, HMS *Cawsand Bay* is pictured here in December 1945. Never commissioned for service, she was laid up in reserve, where she remained until 1959, when she was sent to Genoa to be broken up.

HMS *Vanguard*

Britain's last battleship, pictured here running trials in 1946, she served as a Royal Yacht, as a flagship and with a training squadron. While leaving Portsmouth bound for the scrapyard in 1960 she ran aground, but was pulled clear and sailed to the breaker's yard at Faslane. The largest battleship built for the Royal Navy, she was designed to use mountings for 15-inch guns which had previously been on the battle cruisers HMS *Courageous* and HMS *Glorious* before they were converted to aircraft carriers in the late 1920s. The mounting of the old 15-inch guns on *Vanguard* was done to save time in her construction, by John Brown, Clydebank, and she was launched on 30 November 1944. But she missed seeing combat in the Second World War, as it took until August 1946 for her to be completed. She was used for a royal visit to South Africa in 1947.

HMS *Andrew*

Launched in April 1946, she was one of a class of sixteen boats. She was the last submarine in service with the Royal Navy to carry a gun and in 1953 she had the further distinction of completing the first ever submerged crossing of the Atlantic. She also appeared in a film and a television series, and her final deployment was as a training target for anti-submarine ships. Paid off despite attempts to preserve her, HMS *Andrew* was sold and broken up in Plymouth by Davies and Cann in 1977.

A picture that will evoke many memories, for it shows part of the Reserve Fleet laid up on the Tamar under Brunel's bridge at Saltash.

The destroyers *Fame*, *Hotspur* and *Onslow* on the River Tamar in 1947. *Fame* was to be handed over to the Dominican Navy in 1949, as was the *Hotspur* in 1948, while the *Onslow* went to Pakistan in 1949.

INDEX OF SHIPS

(req. = requisitioned)

SHIP	LAUNCHED	PAGE	SHIP	LAUNCHED	PAGE
Roberts	1941	113	Ullswater	1939	82
Rodney	1925	51	Ulysses	1943	107
Roebuck	1942	136	United	1941	125
Royalist	1942	135			
Royal Oak	1914	31			
			Valiant	1914	43
			Vanguard (1)	1909	33
St Austell Bay	1944	141	Vanguard (2)	1944	153
St Brides Bay	1945	151	Vansittart	1919	65
St George	1892	22	Veryan Bay	1944	143
St Vincent	1815	11			
Sharpshooter	1936	122	Warspite	1913	38
Sirius	1890	19	Watchman	1917	64
Spartan	1942	134	Wellington	1934	83
Speedwell	1889	17	Wolverine	1919	64
Stanley	1940 (req.)	116			
Starling	1942	122			
Stonehenge	1943	127			
Sutton	1918	62			
Switha	1942	104			
Sybille	1890	21			
Talbot	1895	25			
Tally Ho	1942	138			
Tartar	1937	96			
Tavy	1943	137			
Teme	1942	140			
Temeraire	1907	31			
Termagant	1943	120			
Terrible	1944	123			
Thames	1932	89			
Theseus	1892	23			
Thorn	1941	117			
Thunderer	1911	36			
Tiger	1913	40			
Tigris	1939	124			
Titania	1915	48			
Torbay	1940	106			
Torrid	1917	49			
Tremadoc Bay	1945	151			
Trinidad	1940	105			
Thistle	1939	105			
Tyne	1940	111			